Table of Contents

Chapter 1: Understanding Project Management in Mergers and Acquisitions 3
- The Role of Project Management in Mergers and Acquisitions 3
- Overview of Security Department's Involvement in M&A 3
- Importance of Security Professionals in M&A Projects 4

Chapter 2: Integrating Corporate Security Teams in Mergers and Acquisitions 5
- Strategies for Integrating Corporate Security Teams 5
- Challenges in Integrating Security Teams during M&A 6
- Best Practices for Ensuring Smooth Integration of Security Teams 7

Chapter 3: Managing Cyber Security Systems Post-Merger 8
- Assessing Cyber Security Risks Post-Merger 8
- Implementing Cyber Security Policies and Procedures 8
- Coordinating Cyber Security Efforts with Corporate Security Teams 9

Chapter 4: Ensuring Data Security in Mergers and Acquisitions 10
- Strategies for Protecting Data during M&A 10
- Data Security Best Practices 11
- Compliance with Data Privacy Regulations 12

Chapter 5: Coordinating Security Efforts between Corporate and Cyber Security Teams 12
- Communication Strategies for Security Teams 12
- Collaboration Tools for Security Teams 13
- Resolving Conflicts between Corporate and Cyber Security Teams 14

Chapter 6: Transitioning Security Policies and Procedures 15
- Updating Security Policies Post-Merger 15
- Training Employees on New Security Procedures 16
- Ensuring Compliance with Security Protocols 16

Chapter 7: Assessing and Evaluating Security Risks in Mergers and Acquisitions 17
- Conducting Security Risk Assessments 17
- Identifying Vulnerabilities in Security Systems 18
- Mitigating Security Risks during M&A Projects 19

Chapter 8: Implementing a Comprehensive Security Training Program 20
- Developing Security Training Modules 20
- Training Employees on Security Best Practices 21

Monitoring the Effectiveness of Security Training Programs 22

Chapter 9: Consolidating Security Technology and Tools Post-Merger 22

    Evaluating Security Technologies 22

    Integrating Security Tools for Efficiency 23

    Upgrading Security Systems for Enhanced Protection 24

Chapter 10: Strategies for Effective Communication and Collaboration between Security Teams 25

    Establishing Communication Channels 25

    Encouraging Collaboration among Security Teams 26

    Resolving Communication Breakdowns in Security Projects 26

Conclusion: Mastering Project Management in Mergers and Acquisitions for Security Professionals 27

References 28

Chapter 1: Understanding Project Management in Mergers and Acquisitions

The Role of Project Management in Mergers and Acquisitions

Project management plays a crucial role in the success of mergers and acquisitions, particularly in the realm of security. For professionals in project management, mergers and acquisitions, corporate security, and cyber security, understanding how to effectively manage the integration of security teams and systems during a merger or acquisition is essential. This subchapter will delve into the various aspects of project managing mergers and acquisitions for security departments, specifically focusing on corporate security and cyber security.

One of the key challenges in mergers and acquisitions is integrating corporate security teams. Project managers must develop strategies to ensure a smooth transition and collaboration between security professionals from both organizations. This involves aligning security policies, procedures, and technologies to create a unified security framework that addresses the unique risks and threats posed by the merger or acquisition.

In addition to integrating corporate security teams, project managers must also focus on the integration of cyber security systems post-merger. This includes assessing the compatibility of existing cyber security tools and technologies, implementing new security measures to mitigate potential vulnerabilities, and ensuring data security throughout the integration process. Project managers must work closely with cyber security experts to develop a comprehensive strategy for protecting sensitive data and information.

Ensuring data security during a merger or acquisition is paramount in today's digital age. Project managers must prioritize the protection of sensitive information and develop strategies to prevent data breaches and cyber attacks. This may involve conducting security assessments, implementing encryption protocols, and training employees on best practices for data security.

Effective communication and collaboration between corporate and cyber security teams are essential for coordinating security efforts during a merger or acquisition. Project managers must facilitate open dialogue, establish clear channels of communication, and foster a culture of teamwork and cooperation. By promoting collaboration between security teams, project managers can ensure that security measures are effectively implemented and maintained throughout the integration process.

Overview of Security Department's Involvement in M&A

In the realm of mergers and acquisitions, the involvement of the Security Department is crucial to ensuring the successful integration of two entities. This subchapter will provide an overview of the Security Department's role in M&A activities, focusing on how security professionals can effectively manage the various security challenges that arise during this complex process.

One of the key responsibilities of the Security Department during a merger or acquisition is to assess and evaluate security risks. This involves conducting thorough security audits and risk assessments to identify potential vulnerabilities and develop strategies to mitigate them. By proactively addressing security risks, the Security Department can help to safeguard the assets and information of both organizations involved in the M&A deal.

Another important aspect of the Security Department's involvement in M&A is the integration of corporate security teams. This process involves aligning security policies, procedures, and protocols to ensure a seamless transition for employees and stakeholders. By collaborating with corporate security teams, security professionals can create a unified security framework that protects the interests of both organizations post-merger.

In addition to corporate security, cyber security also plays a critical role in M&A activities. Security professionals must project manage the integration of cyber security systems post-merger to ensure the protection of digital assets and data. This includes implementing robust security measures, such as encryption protocols and access controls, to safeguard sensitive information from potential cyber threats.

Furthermore, maintaining data security during a merger or acquisition is paramount to safeguarding the integrity of both organizations. Security professionals must devise strategies for securely transferring and storing data, as well as implementing comprehensive security training programs for employees to educate them on best practices for data protection. By prioritizing data security, security teams can minimize the risk of data breaches and maintain the trust of stakeholders throughout the M&A process.

Overall, effective coordination and collaboration between corporate and cyber security teams are essential for the successful execution of M&A activities. By implementing best practices for security efforts and managing the transition of security policies and procedures, security professionals can ensure a smooth and secure integration process. With a focus on assessing security risks, integrating security teams, and prioritizing data security, security professionals can play a pivotal role in safeguarding the interests of both organizations involved in a merger or acquisition.

Importance of Security Professionals in M&A Projects

In the realm of mergers and acquisitions (M&A), the role of security professionals cannot be overstated. As the guardians of an organization's most valuable assets - its data, infrastructure, and personnel - security professionals play a critical role in ensuring the success and security of M&A projects. In this subchapter, we will delve into the importance of security professionals in M&A projects and highlight the key strategies and best practices for effectively managing security during these complex transitions.

One of the primary reasons why security professionals are indispensable in M&A projects is their expertise in identifying and mitigating security risks. During a merger or acquisition, sensitive information and systems are at risk of being compromised or exploited. Security professionals possess the knowledge and skills to assess these risks, develop comprehensive security strategies, and implement robust protective measures to safeguard the organization's assets.

Furthermore, security professionals are instrumental in facilitating the integration of corporate security teams during a merger or acquisition. By collaborating with key stakeholders and aligning security policies and procedures, security professionals can ensure a seamless transition and minimize disruptions to business operations. This coordination is crucial in maintaining the security posture of the organization and mitigating potential vulnerabilities during the integration process.

In addition to corporate security, security professionals also play a pivotal role in managing the integration of cyber security systems post-merger. With the increasing threat of cyber attacks and data breaches, it is imperative for organizations to fortify their cyber defenses and ensure the secure transfer of data and information. Security professionals are well-equipped to assess the existing cyber security infrastructure, identify gaps, and implement effective measures to protect against potential threats.

Moreover, security professionals are essential in implementing a comprehensive security training program for employees post-merger. By educating staff on security best practices, protocols, and procedures, security professionals can enhance the organization's overall security awareness and resilience. This training is crucial in fostering a culture of security and empowering employees to play an active role in safeguarding the organization's assets.

Overall, the contribution of security professionals in M&A projects cannot be underestimated. By leveraging their expertise, experience, and strategic insights, security professionals can help organizations navigate the complexities of mergers and acquisitions, safeguard their assets, and ensure a smooth and secure transition. For professionals in project management, mergers and acquisitions, corporate security, and cyber security, mastering the role of security professionals in M&A projects is essential for driving success and resilience in today's dynamic business environment.

Chapter 2: Integrating Corporate Security Teams in Mergers and Acquisitions

Strategies for Integrating Corporate Security Teams

In the process of integrating corporate security teams during a merger or acquisition, it is essential to have a well-thought-out strategy in place. This subchapter will outline key strategies that security professionals can implement to ensure a smooth transition and effective collaboration between corporate security and cyber security teams.

One of the first strategies to consider is establishing clear communication channels between the two teams. This includes regular meetings, updates on project milestones, and a shared project management platform. By maintaining open lines of communication, both teams can stay informed and aligned on the integration process.

Another important strategy is to conduct a thorough assessment of security risks during the merger or acquisition. This involves identifying potential vulnerabilities, assessing the impact of the merger on current security measures, and developing a plan to mitigate any risks. By proactively addressing security concerns, the teams can prevent potential breaches or data loss during the integration process.

To ensure data security during a merger or acquisition, it is crucial to implement strict access controls and data encryption protocols. This includes restricting access to sensitive information, monitoring data transfers, and encrypting data both in transit and at rest. By prioritizing data security, the teams can safeguard critical information and prevent unauthorized access.

In addition to technical measures, it is also important to focus on training and education for employees post-merger. This includes providing security awareness training, updating security policies and procedures, and ensuring that all employees understand their role in maintaining a secure environment. By investing in comprehensive security training, the teams can build a culture of security awareness within the organization.

Overall, by following these strategies for integrating corporate security teams during a merger or acquisition, security professionals can effectively manage the transition, mitigate security risks, and ensure a secure environment for the newly merged organization. By prioritizing communication, risk assessment, data security, and employee training, the teams can work together seamlessly to protect the organization from potential threats and vulnerabilities.

Challenges in Integrating Security Teams during M&A

Integrating security teams during a merger or acquisition presents a unique set of challenges for professionals in project management, corporate security, and cyber security. One of the primary obstacles is the clash of cultures and processes between the two organizations. Corporate security teams may have different protocols and procedures than their counterparts in cyber security, leading to confusion and inefficiencies in the integration process. Additionally, there may be resistance from employees who are hesitant to change their established security practices.

Another challenge in integrating security teams during M&A is the issue of data security. With the influx of new systems and technologies, there is a risk of vulnerabilities and breaches if security measures are not properly implemented. It is essential for project managers to work closely with both corporate and cyber security teams to ensure that data security is prioritized throughout the integration process. This may involve conducting risk assessments, implementing new security protocols, and providing comprehensive training for employees on best practices for data protection.

Communication and collaboration between security teams can also be a significant challenge during a merger or acquisition. Different departments may have varying priorities and objectives, making it difficult to align on security strategies and initiatives. Project managers must facilitate effective communication channels and establish clear lines of responsibility to ensure that security efforts are coordinated and cohesive. This may involve creating cross-functional teams, holding regular meetings, and providing regular updates on security progress.

Managing the transition of security policies and procedures is another critical aspect of integrating security teams during M&A. It is essential to evaluate the existing policies of both organizations, identify gaps and redundancies, and develop a unified set of security protocols that align with the new company's objectives. Project managers must ensure that these policies are communicated effectively to employees and that compliance is enforced throughout the organization.

In conclusion, integrating security teams during a merger or acquisition requires careful planning, communication, and coordination. By addressing challenges such as cultural differences, data security, communication barriers, and policy transitions, project managers can ensure a smooth and successful integration process. By following best practices and strategies for coordinating security efforts between corporate and cyber security teams, organizations can enhance their security posture and minimize risks during times of change and transition.

Best Practices for Ensuring Smooth Integration of Security Teams

In order to ensure a smooth integration of security teams during a merger or acquisition, it is essential for professionals in project management, corporate security, and cyber security to follow best practices that will help facilitate collaboration and coordination. One key practice is to establish clear communication channels between all security teams involved in the merger or acquisition. This includes regular meetings, updates on progress, and sharing of important information to ensure alignment and understanding of goals and objectives.

Another important aspect to consider is the coordination of security efforts between corporate security and cyber security teams. By creating a unified approach to security, organizations can address potential vulnerabilities and threats more effectively. This may involve aligning security policies and procedures, sharing resources, and developing strategies to mitigate risks and protect sensitive data.

Project managing the integration of cyber security systems post-merger is also crucial in ensuring a secure transition. This includes conducting thorough assessments of existing systems, evaluating potential risks, and implementing necessary upgrades or changes to enhance security measures. It is imperative to involve both corporate security and cyber security teams in this process to ensure a comprehensive and cohesive approach.

Managing the transition of security policies and procedures during a merger or acquisition requires careful planning and coordination. This may involve revising existing policies to align with the new organizational structure, communicating changes to all employees, and providing training on updated procedures. By implementing a comprehensive security training program for employees post-merger, organizations can ensure that all staff are equipped with the knowledge and skills to protect sensitive information and prevent security breaches.

Lastly, implementing a strategy for effective communication and collaboration between security teams is essential for the success of the integration process. This may involve creating cross-functional teams, establishing regular reporting mechanisms, and fostering a culture of transparency and cooperation. By following these best practices, professionals in project management, corporate security, and cyber security can navigate the complexities of mergers and acquisitions with confidence and ensure the security of their organizations' assets and data.

Chapter 3: Managing Cyber Security Systems Post-Merger

Assessing Cyber Security Risks Post-Merger

In the realm of project management for mergers and acquisitions, one critical aspect that cannot be overlooked is the assessment of cyber security risks post-merger. As security professionals, it is imperative that we understand the potential vulnerabilities that may arise as a result of the integration of two separate entities. By conducting a thorough assessment of cyber security risks, we can identify areas of concern and develop strategies to mitigate these risks effectively.

When assessing cyber security risks post-merger, it is essential to consider factors such as the compatibility of existing security systems, the potential for data breaches, and the vulnerability of critical assets. By conducting a comprehensive evaluation of these factors, security professionals can gain a clear understanding of the potential risks that may arise during the integration process. This knowledge is crucial for developing a robust security strategy that can effectively protect the merged entity from cyber threats.

One key aspect of assessing cyber security risks post-merger is the integration of corporate security teams. By bringing together security professionals from both entities, organizations can leverage their collective expertise to identify and address potential vulnerabilities. This collaborative approach can help ensure that the merged entity is well-equipped to handle any cyber security challenges that may arise during the integration process.

Another important consideration when assessing cyber security risks post-merger is the implementation of a comprehensive security training program for employees. By educating staff members about best practices for data security and cyber hygiene, organizations can help mitigate the risk of human error leading to security breaches. This training program should be tailored to the specific needs of the merged entity and should be regularly updated to address new threats and vulnerabilities.

In conclusion, assessing cyber security risks post-merger is a critical step in the project management process for mergers and acquisitions. By conducting a thorough evaluation of potential vulnerabilities, integrating corporate security teams, implementing a comprehensive security training program, and developing strategies to mitigate risks, security professionals can help ensure that the merged entity is well-protected against cyber threats. By taking a proactive approach to cyber security, organizations can minimize the risk of data breaches and other security incidents, ultimately safeguarding their reputation and bottom line.

Implementing Cyber Security Policies and Procedures

Implementing Cyber Security Policies and Procedures is a critical aspect of project managing mergers and acquisitions, especially for professionals in the fields of corporate security and cyber security. In order to ensure a smooth transition and integration of security measures post-merger, it is essential to establish clear and comprehensive policies and procedures that address the unique challenges and risks associated with combining two organizations.

One of the first steps in implementing cyber security policies and procedures during a merger or acquisition is to conduct a thorough assessment and evaluation of the existing security infrastructure and risks. This will help identify any gaps or vulnerabilities that need to be addressed in order to protect sensitive data and information. By understanding the current state of security within both organizations, security professionals can develop a strategic plan for integrating security systems and technologies post-merger.

Another key aspect of implementing cyber security policies and procedures is coordinating efforts between corporate security and cyber security teams. Collaboration and communication between these two departments are essential for ensuring a seamless transition and alignment of security measures. By establishing a clear framework for sharing information and collaborating on security initiatives, organizations can effectively manage the integration of security systems and technologies post-merger.

Furthermore, managing the transition of security policies and procedures during a merger or acquisition requires a comprehensive approach that takes into account the unique needs and challenges of both organizations. This may involve consolidating security technology and tools, implementing new training programs for employees, and developing strategies for ensuring data security throughout the integration process. By proactively addressing these issues, security professionals can mitigate potential risks and ensure a secure and resilient security infrastructure post-merger.

In conclusion, implementing cyber security policies and procedures is a critical component of project managing mergers and acquisitions for security professionals. By conducting thorough assessments, coordinating efforts between corporate security and cyber security teams, and managing the transition of security policies and procedures, organizations can effectively protect sensitive data and information during a merger or acquisition. By following best practices and strategies for integrating security measures post-merger, security professionals can ensure a smooth and secure transition for their organizations.

Coordinating Cyber Security Efforts with Corporate Security Teams

In the realm of mergers and acquisitions, the coordination of cyber security efforts with corporate security teams is paramount to ensuring a smooth transition and safeguarding sensitive information. For professionals in project management, Mergers and acquisitions, Corporate Security, and Cyber Security, the integration of these two crucial departments can be a complex and challenging task. However, with the right strategies and best practices in place, the process can be managed effectively to mitigate risks and ensure the security of all systems and data.

One key aspect of coordinating cyber security efforts with corporate security teams during a merger or acquisition is the alignment of security policies and procedures. It is essential to conduct a thorough assessment and evaluation of security risks to identify any vulnerabilities and establish a comprehensive security framework that addresses the unique needs of the combined organization. This process requires meticulous project management to ensure that all security measures are implemented seamlessly and efficiently.

Another critical component of integrating corporate security teams during a merger or acquisition is the consolidation of security technology and tools. This involves assessing the existing security infrastructure of both organizations and identifying redundancies or gaps that need to be addressed. By project managing the consolidation of security technology, teams can streamline operations, reduce costs, and enhance overall security posture.

Furthermore, effective communication and collaboration between security teams are essential for success in coordinating cyber security efforts with corporate security teams. Clear and open lines of communication facilitate the sharing of information, best practices, and insights that are crucial for identifying and addressing security threats. Project managers play a vital role in fostering collaboration and ensuring that all team members are working towards a common goal of protecting the organization's assets.

Lastly, implementing a comprehensive security training program for employees post-merger is vital to creating a culture of security awareness and compliance. Project managing the development and delivery of security training ensures that all staff members are equipped with the knowledge and skills to safeguard sensitive information and mitigate security risks. By investing in security education, organizations can strengthen their defenses and reduce the likelihood of security incidents during the integration process.

Chapter 4: Ensuring Data Security in Mergers and Acquisitions

Strategies for Protecting Data during M&A

In the fast-paced world of mergers and acquisitions, security professionals play a crucial role in safeguarding sensitive data and protecting valuable assets. To ensure the success of a merger or acquisition, it is essential to implement effective strategies for protecting data during this transitional period. This subchapter will explore key strategies for professionals in project management, mergers and acquisitions, corporate security, and cyber security to consider when navigating the complexities of data security in M&A transactions.

One of the first steps in protecting data during a merger or acquisition is to conduct a thorough risk assessment. This involves identifying potential vulnerabilities and assessing the potential impact of a data breach on the organization. By understanding the risks involved, security professionals can develop a comprehensive security plan that addresses any potential threats and vulnerabilities.

Once potential risks have been identified, it is important to implement robust security measures to protect sensitive data. This may include encryption, access controls, and monitoring systems to detect and prevent unauthorized access to critical information. By implementing these security measures, organizations can mitigate the risk of a data breach and protect their valuable assets during the M&A process.

Effective communication and collaboration between corporate security and cyber security teams are also essential for protecting data during a merger or acquisition. By fostering open lines of communication and working together to address security concerns, organizations can ensure that data security remains a top priority throughout the M&A process. This collaboration can also help to streamline security efforts and ensure that all security measures are implemented effectively.

Finally, it is important to continuously evaluate and update security policies and procedures to adapt to the changing landscape of a merged or acquired organization. By regularly assessing security risks and updating security measures as needed, organizations can stay ahead of potential threats and protect their data from unauthorized access. By following these strategies and best practices, security professionals can help to ensure the success of a merger or acquisition while safeguarding valuable data and assets.

Data Security Best Practices

Data security is a critical aspect of any merger or acquisition, as sensitive information is often at risk during these transitional periods. In order to ensure the protection of valuable data, it is essential for professionals in project management, mergers and acquisitions, corporate security, and cyber security to follow best practices for data security.

One of the key best practices for data security during a merger or acquisition is to conduct a thorough assessment of security risks. This involves identifying potential vulnerabilities and threats to the organization's data, as well as evaluating the effectiveness of current security measures. By understanding the risks involved, security professionals can develop strategies to mitigate these threats and protect sensitive information.

In addition to assessing security risks, it is important to coordinate security efforts between corporate and cyber security teams. This involves effective communication and collaboration between the two teams to ensure that security measures are aligned and integrated seamlessly. By working together, security professionals can maximize the effectiveness of their security efforts and minimize the risk of data breaches.

Another best practice for data security during a merger or acquisition is to implement a comprehensive security training program for employees. This involves educating staff members on the importance of data security, as well as providing them with the knowledge and skills they need to protect sensitive information. By investing in employee training, organizations can strengthen their overall security posture and reduce the likelihood of data breaches.

Finally, it is essential to manage the consolidation of security technology and tools post-merger. This involves evaluating the organization's existing security infrastructure, identifying redundancies and inefficiencies, and implementing a streamlined and integrated security system.

By consolidating security technology and tools, organizations can improve their overall security posture and better protect their data during the merger or acquisition process.

Compliance with Data Privacy Regulations

Compliance with data privacy regulations is a critical aspect of project management in mergers and acquisitions, especially for security professionals. Ensuring that data is handled in accordance with relevant laws and regulations is essential to protecting sensitive information and maintaining the trust of stakeholders. In this subchapter, we will explore the importance of data privacy compliance and provide guidance on how to navigate this complex landscape.

One of the key challenges in managing data privacy during a merger or acquisition is ensuring that all parties involved understand and adhere to relevant regulations. This may involve conducting thorough audits of existing data practices, identifying potential risks, and implementing robust data protection measures. Security professionals play a crucial role in guiding these efforts and ensuring that data privacy considerations are integrated into all aspects of the project.

In addition to legal compliance, security professionals must also consider the ethical implications of data privacy during a merger or acquisition. This may involve balancing the need for transparency with the need to protect sensitive information, as well as ensuring that data is used responsibly and in accordance with the expectations of stakeholders. By making ethical considerations a priority, security professionals can help build trust and credibility within the organization.

Effective communication and collaboration between corporate security and cyber security teams are essential for ensuring data privacy compliance during a merger or acquisition. By working together to identify risks, develop mitigation strategies, and monitor compliance, security professionals can help ensure that data is protected throughout the project. This may involve establishing clear lines of communication, coordinating efforts, and sharing information to address potential vulnerabilities.

Ultimately, compliance with data privacy regulations is not only a legal requirement but also a critical component of maintaining the security and integrity of an organization. By prioritizing data privacy, security professionals can help mitigate risks, build trust with stakeholders, and ensure the success of mergers and acquisitions. By following best practices and staying informed about evolving regulations, security professionals can navigate the complex landscape of data privacy with confidence and competence.

Chapter 5: Coordinating Security Efforts between Corporate and Cyber Security Teams

Communication Strategies for Security Teams

Communication is a vital aspect of project management in the context of mergers and acquisitions, especially when it comes to security teams. Effective communication strategies are essential for ensuring a smooth transition and integration of security processes during a merger or acquisition. For professionals in project management, Mergers and acquisitions, Corporate Security, and Cyber Security, it is crucial to establish clear lines of communication between all security teams involved in the process.

One key communication strategy for security teams during a merger or acquisition is regular and transparent updates on the progress of security integration. This helps keep all team members informed about the changes happening within the organization and allows for any potential issues to be addressed in a timely manner. It is important for project managers to establish a communication plan that outlines how and when updates will be shared with the security teams.

Another important aspect of communication strategy for security teams is the coordination of efforts between corporate security and cyber security teams. Ensuring that both teams are aligned in their goals and strategies is essential for maintaining a high level of security throughout the merger or acquisition process. Project managers should facilitate regular meetings and discussions between the two teams to ensure that they are working together effectively.

In addition to coordinating efforts between corporate security and cyber security teams, project managers should also focus on ensuring data security during a merger or acquisition. This includes implementing secure data transfer protocols, conducting regular security audits, and training employees on best practices for data protection. Communication plays a crucial role in ensuring that all team members are aware of the importance of data security and are actively working towards maintaining it.

Overall, effective communication strategies for security teams during a merger or acquisition are essential for the success of the project. By establishing clear lines of communication, coordinating efforts between different security teams, and focusing on data security, project managers can ensure a smooth transition and integration of security processes. It is important for professionals in project management, Mergers and acquisitions, Corporate Security, and Cyber Security to prioritize communication and collaboration between security teams to achieve successful outcomes.

Collaboration Tools for Security Teams

In the fast-paced world of mergers and acquisitions, security professionals play a crucial role in ensuring the safety and integrity of the organizations involved. Collaboration tools can significantly enhance the effectiveness and efficiency of security teams during these complex processes. In this subchapter, we will explore some of the key collaboration tools that can help security professionals navigate the challenges of managing security in mergers and acquisitions.

One essential collaboration tool for security teams is a secure communication platform. This tool allows team members to securely communicate and share important information, such as threat alerts, incident reports, and security policies. By centralizing communication in a secure platform, security teams can ensure that sensitive information remains confidential and accessible only to authorized personnel.

Another valuable collaboration tool for security teams is a project management software. This tool can help security professionals streamline the planning, execution, and monitoring of security initiatives during mergers and acquisitions. With features such as task assignment, progress tracking, and deadline reminders, project management software can help security teams stay organized and focused on their objectives.

Collaboration tools for security teams can also include virtual collaboration platforms, which enable team members to collaborate in real-time regardless of their physical location. These platforms allow security professionals to conduct virtual meetings, share documents, and collaborate on projects in a secure online environment. By leveraging virtual collaboration tools, security teams can work together seamlessly, even when they are geographically dispersed.

In conclusion, collaboration tools are essential for security teams to effectively manage the complexities of mergers and acquisitions. By utilizing secure communication platforms, project management software, and virtual collaboration platforms, security professionals can enhance their ability to protect the organizations they serve. As the landscape of corporate security and cyber security continues to evolve, investing in collaboration tools is crucial for security teams to stay ahead of potential threats and challenges.

Resolving Conflicts between Corporate and Cyber Security Teams

In the fast-paced world of mergers and acquisitions, conflicts between corporate and cyber security teams can often arise. These conflicts can stem from differences in priorities, communication breakdowns, or simply a lack of understanding of each team's role and responsibilities. As professionals in project management, mergers and acquisitions, corporate security, and cyber security, it is crucial to address these conflicts head-on and find effective solutions to ensure the security of all parties involved.

One key strategy for resolving conflicts between corporate and cyber security teams is to establish clear lines of communication and collaboration. By fostering open and transparent communication channels, both teams can better understand each other's goals and work together towards a common objective. Regular meetings, brainstorming sessions, and workshops can help bridge the gap between corporate and cyber security teams and facilitate the sharing of knowledge and expertise.

Another important aspect of resolving conflicts between corporate and cyber security teams is to create a unified security strategy that takes into account the unique needs and challenges of both teams. This can involve developing a comprehensive security policy that outlines the roles and responsibilities of each team, as well as implementing specific protocols and procedures for handling security incidents and breaches. By aligning their goals and objectives, corporate and cyber security teams can work together more effectively and efficiently to protect the organization's assets and data.

Furthermore, it is essential to establish a clear chain of command and decision-making process to ensure that conflicts between corporate and cyber security teams are resolved in a timely and effective manner. By assigning specific roles and responsibilities to key stakeholders within each team, such as project managers, security analysts, and IT professionals, decisions can be made quickly and efficiently, minimizing the impact of conflicts on the organization's security posture.

Overall, by proactively addressing conflicts between corporate and cyber security teams through effective communication, collaboration, and a unified security strategy, professionals in project management, mergers and acquisitions, corporate security, and cyber security can ensure the successful integration of security efforts during a merger or acquisition. By working together towards a common goal of protecting the organization's assets and data, these teams can overcome conflicts and challenges to create a secure and resilient security environment post-merger.

Chapter 6: Transitioning Security Policies and Procedures

Updating Security Policies Post-Merger

Updating security policies post-merger is a critical task that should not be overlooked in the integration process. As professionals in project management, mergers and acquisitions, corporate security, and cyber security, it is essential to ensure that the security of the newly formed entity is not compromised during the transition period. This subchapter will discuss best practices for updating security policies post-merger to safeguard the organization's assets and data.

One of the key aspects of updating security policies post-merger is to conduct a thorough assessment of the existing security policies and procedures of both organizations. This will help identify any gaps or inconsistencies that need to be addressed in the new security framework. By evaluating the security risks and vulnerabilities of the merged entity, security professionals can develop a comprehensive plan to enhance the security posture and mitigate potential threats.

Another important consideration when updating security policies post-merger is to ensure that all employees are aware of the changes and are trained on the new security protocols. Implementing a comprehensive security training program for employees post-merger will help foster a culture of security awareness and compliance within the organization. By educating employees on the importance of adhering to security policies, the risk of human error or negligence can be minimized.

In addition to training employees, it is crucial to coordinate security efforts between corporate and cyber security teams during a merger or acquisition. By establishing clear lines of communication and collaboration between these teams, security professionals can work together to address security challenges and implement effective security measures. This collaboration will help ensure a seamless integration of security processes and technologies post-merger.

Overall, updating security policies post-merger requires a strategic and coordinated approach to protect the organization from potential security threats. By following best practices for integrating security teams, assessing security risks, implementing training programs, and fostering collaboration between corporate and cyber security teams, security professionals can effectively manage the transition of security policies and procedures during a merger or acquisition.

Training Employees on New Security Procedures

Training employees on new security procedures is a crucial aspect of successfully integrating corporate security teams during a merger or acquisition. As professionals in project management, mergers and acquisitions, corporate security, and cyber security, it is essential to ensure that all employees are well-versed in the latest security protocols to protect the organization from potential threats. This subchapter will outline the best practices for implementing a comprehensive security training program for employees post-merger, as well as strategies for coordinating security efforts between corporate and cyber security teams.

One of the first steps in training employees on new security procedures is to assess the existing knowledge and skills of the workforce. This can be done through surveys, interviews, or assessments to identify any gaps in understanding. Once these gaps are identified, a customized training program can be developed to address the specific needs of the employees. This may include in-person training sessions, online courses, or workshops to educate employees on the importance of security protocols and how to effectively implement them in their daily tasks.

Effective communication and collaboration between security teams are essential during a merger or acquisition to ensure a smooth transition and integration of security procedures. Project managers should facilitate regular meetings between corporate security and cyber security teams to discuss any updates or changes to security protocols. This allows for a cohesive approach to security management and ensures that all teams are working towards the same goal of protecting the organization from potential threats.

In addition to training employees on new security procedures, it is also important to manage the transition of security policies and procedures during a merger or acquisition. This may involve updating existing policies, creating new guidelines, or implementing additional security measures to address any vulnerabilities that may arise from the merger. Project managers should work closely with security teams to ensure that all policies and procedures are aligned with the organization's overall security strategy and goals.

Overall, implementing a comprehensive security training program for employees post-merger is essential for the success of the integration of corporate security teams. By coordinating security efforts between corporate and cyber security teams, managing the transition of security policies and procedures, and fostering effective communication and collaboration, organizations can mitigate security risks and protect sensitive data during a merger or acquisition.

Ensuring Compliance with Security Protocols

Ensuring compliance with security protocols is paramount when managing mergers and acquisitions in today's fast-paced business environment. For professionals in project management, mergers and acquisitions, corporate security, and cyber security, it is crucial to establish and maintain a robust framework for security protocols to safeguard sensitive data and protect organizational assets.

Integrating corporate security teams during a merger or acquisition requires careful planning and coordination. Project managers must work closely with security professionals to ensure a seamless transition and alignment of security policies and procedures. This includes conducting thorough risk assessments and evaluations to identify potential vulnerabilities and threats that may arise during the integration process.

Project managing the integration of cyber security systems post-merger is essential for safeguarding digital assets and preventing cyber threats. This involves consolidating security technology and tools to create a unified and comprehensive security infrastructure. By implementing a comprehensive security training program for employees post-merger, organizations can enhance awareness and ensure adherence to security protocols across all levels of the organization.

Strategies for ensuring data security during a merger or acquisition include establishing clear guidelines for data protection, encryption, and access control. Project managers must collaborate with both corporate and cyber security teams to coordinate efforts and address any security gaps that may arise during the integration process. Effective communication and collaboration between security teams are key to mitigating risks and ensuring a smooth transition.

Managing the transition of security policies and procedures during a merger or acquisition requires a proactive approach and a focus on compliance with industry regulations and best practices. By aligning security efforts and implementing robust security measures, organizations can minimize security risks and protect their assets from potential threats. With a strategic and coordinated approach to security management, professionals can navigate the complexities of mergers and acquisitions while safeguarding their organization's security posture.

Chapter 7: Assessing and Evaluating Security Risks in Mergers and Acquisitions

Conducting Security Risk Assessments

Conducting security risk assessments is a crucial step in the process of project managing mergers and acquisitions, especially for security professionals involved in corporate security and cyber security. By evaluating potential risks and vulnerabilities, security teams can identify areas of concern and develop strategies to mitigate these risks effectively. This subchapter will provide insights into the best practices for conducting security risk assessments during mergers and acquisitions, with a focus on integrating corporate security teams and cyber security systems, ensuring data security, coordinating security efforts between teams, managing security policies and procedures, and evaluating security risks.

One of the key aspects of conducting security risk assessments during mergers and acquisitions is the integration of corporate security teams. It is essential for security professionals to collaborate and communicate effectively with their counterparts in the organization being acquired or merged with. By sharing information and resources, security teams can align their strategies and ensure a seamless transition of security operations. This collaboration also helps in identifying potential gaps or weaknesses in existing security measures and developing a comprehensive security plan for the combined entity.

In addition to integrating corporate security teams, it is equally important to manage the integration of cyber security systems post-merger. This involves evaluating the existing cyber security infrastructure, identifying potential vulnerabilities, and implementing necessary upgrades or changes to enhance the overall security posture of the organization. By conducting a thorough assessment of cyber security systems, security professionals can ensure the protection of critical data and information assets during the merger or acquisition process.

To ensure data security during mergers and acquisitions, security professionals must develop strategies to safeguard sensitive information from potential threats. This includes implementing encryption protocols, access controls, and monitoring mechanisms to prevent unauthorized access or data breaches. By establishing robust data security measures, security teams can protect the confidentiality, integrity, and availability of data throughout the merger or acquisition process.

Moreover, coordinating security efforts between corporate security and cyber security teams is essential for a successful merger or acquisition. By aligning their strategies and resources, security professionals can effectively address security challenges and mitigate risks. Regular communication and collaboration between teams help in identifying emerging threats, sharing best practices, and implementing consistent security measures across the organization. This synergistic approach ensures a unified front against security threats and enhances the overall security posture of the merged entity.

Identifying Vulnerabilities in Security Systems

In the world of project management in mergers and acquisitions, one of the crucial aspects that security professionals must focus on is identifying vulnerabilities in security systems. This subchapter will delve into the importance of recognizing weaknesses in security systems and the strategies for addressing them effectively.

To begin with, it is essential for security professionals to conduct a thorough assessment of the existing security systems in place before, during, and after a merger or acquisition. This involves identifying potential gaps, loopholes, and vulnerabilities that could be exploited by cybercriminals or malicious actors. By conducting a comprehensive security audit, security professionals can proactively address any weaknesses and strengthen the overall security posture of the organization.

Furthermore, security professionals must pay close attention to the integration of corporate security teams during a merger or acquisition. It is crucial to ensure that all security personnel are aligned in their objectives and have a unified approach to addressing security concerns. By fostering collaboration and communication between corporate security teams, security professionals can effectively mitigate security risks and enhance overall security resilience.

In addition to corporate security, the integration of cyber security systems post-merger is equally important. Security professionals must carefully evaluate the compatibility of existing cyber security systems and technologies to identify any potential vulnerabilities or gaps. By conducting a thorough assessment of cyber security systems, security professionals can implement robust security measures to safeguard sensitive data and prevent cyber threats.

Moreover, security professionals must develop strategies for ensuring data security during a merger or acquisition. This involves implementing encryption protocols, access controls, and data protection measures to safeguard confidential information from unauthorized access or disclosure. By prioritizing data security, security professionals can minimize the risk of data breaches and protect the organization's reputation and financial assets.

In conclusion, identifying vulnerabilities in security systems is a critical aspect of project management in mergers and acquisitions for security professionals. By conducting thorough assessments, integrating corporate and cyber security teams, implementing robust security measures, and prioritizing data security, security professionals can effectively mitigate security risks and safeguard the organization's assets during a merger or acquisition.

Mitigating Security Risks during M&A Projects

Mitigating security risks during M&A projects is a critical aspect of the overall integration process. As professionals in project management, mergers and acquisitions, corporate security, and cyber security, it is imperative to have a comprehensive understanding of the potential risks and challenges that may arise during these complex transactions. By proactively identifying and addressing security risks, organizations can minimize the likelihood of data breaches, cyber attacks, and other security incidents that could have a detrimental impact on the success of the merger or acquisition.

One key strategy for mitigating security risks during M&A projects is to integrate corporate security teams early in the process. By involving security professionals from both organizations in the due diligence and planning phases, potential vulnerabilities can be identified and addressed before they become a threat. This collaboration allows for a more holistic approach to security risk management and ensures that all aspects of security are taken into consideration throughout the integration process.

Another important consideration for security professionals during M&A projects is the integration of cyber security systems post-merger. This includes assessing the compatibility of existing systems, implementing necessary updates or upgrades, and developing a unified approach to monitoring and protecting sensitive data. By aligning cyber security efforts, organizations can strengthen their defenses against potential threats and enhance overall security posture.

Ensuring data security during a merger or acquisition is also crucial for protecting sensitive information and maintaining compliance with regulatory requirements. Security professionals should develop a comprehensive data security strategy that includes encryption, access controls, and monitoring mechanisms to safeguard critical data assets. By implementing robust data security measures, organizations can minimize the risk of data breaches and unauthorized access to confidential information.

Effective communication and collaboration between corporate and cyber security teams are essential for coordinating security efforts during a merger or acquisition. By establishing clear lines of communication, sharing information about potential risks, and collaborating on security strategies, organizations can enhance their overall security posture and minimize the impact of security incidents. By following best practices and leveraging the expertise of security professionals, organizations can successfully navigate the complexities of M&A projects while mitigating security risks and ensuring the protection of critical assets.

Chapter 8: Implementing a Comprehensive Security Training Program

Developing Security Training Modules

Developing Security Training Modules is a crucial aspect of successfully managing mergers and acquisitions within the realm of corporate and cyber security. These modules serve as a foundational tool for educating employees on new security policies and procedures, as well as integrating security teams during a transition period. In order to effectively implement these training modules, it is essential to follow a strategic approach that aligns with the overall project management goals of the merger or acquisition.

First and foremost, security professionals must conduct a thorough assessment of the existing security training programs within both organizations involved in the merger or acquisition. This evaluation will help identify any gaps or redundancies in training content, as well as areas where additional training may be necessary. By understanding the current state of security training, professionals can develop targeted modules that address specific needs and ensure a seamless integration process.

Once the assessment phase is complete, the next step is to design customized security training modules that are tailored to the unique needs of the newly merged or acquired organization. These modules should cover a range of topics, including data security best practices, compliance requirements, and incident response protocols. By developing comprehensive training materials, security professionals can ensure that employees are equipped with the knowledge and skills needed to protect sensitive information and mitigate security risks.

In addition to content development, security professionals must also consider the delivery methods for these training modules. Whether through in-person workshops, online courses, or interactive simulations, it is important to choose a format that resonates with employees and promotes engagement. By incorporating a variety of training techniques, professionals can ensure that employees retain key security concepts and are motivated to apply them in their daily work.

Finally, ongoing evaluation and feedback are essential components of developing effective security training modules. By regularly assessing the impact of the training program and soliciting input from employees, security professionals can make necessary adjustments and improvements to ensure continued success. By prioritizing the development of security training modules, professionals can strengthen the overall security posture of the organization and mitigate potential risks during a merger or acquisition.

Training Employees on Security Best Practices

Training employees on security best practices is crucial during a merger or acquisition to ensure that sensitive data and information are protected. As professionals in project management, Mergers and acquisitions, Corporate Security, and Cyber Security, it is essential to implement a comprehensive security training program for all employees post-merger. This training should cover topics such as identifying phishing scams, creating strong passwords, recognizing social engineering tactics, and understanding the importance of data encryption.

To effectively train employees on security best practices, it is important to tailor the training to the specific needs and challenges of the organization post-merger. This may involve conducting a thorough assessment and evaluation of security risks to determine the areas where employees need the most guidance. By customizing the training program to address these specific risks, employees will be better equipped to protect sensitive information and prevent security breaches.

In addition to providing employees with the knowledge and skills they need to protect company data, it is also important to ensure that they understand the importance of adhering to security policies and procedures. Project managing the transition of security policies and procedures during a merger or acquisition can help to ensure that all employees are aware of the expectations and requirements for maintaining a secure work environment. This may involve updating existing policies, creating new protocols, and conducting regular training sessions to reinforce these guidelines.

Furthermore, coordinating security efforts between corporate and cyber security teams is essential for a successful merger or acquisition. By implementing strategies for effective communication and collaboration between these teams, professionals can ensure that all aspects of security are being addressed in a coordinated and cohesive manner. By working together to identify potential vulnerabilities and develop comprehensive security solutions, corporate and cyber security teams can protect the organization from external threats and internal risks.

Overall, implementing a robust security training program for employees post-merger is a critical step in protecting the organization from security breaches and data leaks. By project managing the integration of security best practices, policies, and procedures, professionals can ensure that all employees are equipped with the knowledge and skills they need to maintain a secure work environment. By fostering collaboration between corporate and cyber security teams and emphasizing the importance of following security protocols, organizations can minimize the risks associated with a merger or acquisition and safeguard their valuable assets.

Monitoring the Effectiveness of Security Training Programs

Monitoring the effectiveness of security training programs is crucial in ensuring that employees are equipped with the knowledge and skills necessary to protect the organization during a merger or acquisition. As professionals in project management, mergers and acquisitions, corporate security, and cyber security, it is essential to establish metrics and processes for evaluating the impact of security training initiatives.

One key aspect of monitoring the effectiveness of security training programs is setting clear objectives and goals for what the training should achieve. These objectives should be aligned with the overall security strategy of the organization and should be measurable in order to track progress and success. By clearly defining what success looks like, organizations can better assess the impact of their training efforts.

In addition to setting clear objectives, it is important to gather feedback from employees who have completed security training programs. This feedback can provide valuable insights into the effectiveness of the training, including what worked well and what areas may need improvement. By soliciting feedback from employees, organizations can continuously refine and enhance their security training programs to better meet the needs of staff.

Another important element of monitoring the effectiveness of security training programs is conducting regular assessments and evaluations. These assessments can help identify gaps in knowledge or areas where additional training may be needed. By regularly evaluating the impact of security training programs, organizations can ensure that their employees are well-prepared to handle security threats during a merger or acquisition.

Ultimately, monitoring the effectiveness of security training programs requires a proactive and ongoing approach. By establishing clear objectives, gathering feedback from employees, and conducting regular assessments, organizations can ensure that their security training initiatives are meeting the needs of employees and effectively preparing them to protect the organization during a merger or acquisition.

Chapter 9: Consolidating Security Technology and Tools Post-Merger

Evaluating Security Technologies

When evaluating security technologies during a merger or acquisition, it is crucial for professionals in project management, corporate security, and cyber security to have a thorough understanding of the existing systems in place. This involves conducting a comprehensive assessment of the current security infrastructure, including hardware, software, and protocols. By identifying any vulnerabilities or weaknesses in the systems, security professionals can develop a strategic plan for integrating new technologies post-merger.

One key aspect of evaluating security technologies is determining the compatibility of existing systems with those of the acquiring company. This may involve conducting compatibility tests and assessments to ensure a seamless integration of security technologies. It is important for security professionals to collaborate closely with IT and technology teams to identify any potential roadblocks and develop solutions to mitigate risks during the integration process.

In addition to compatibility, security professionals must also consider the scalability and flexibility of security technologies. As the merged entity grows and evolves, the security infrastructure must be able to adapt to changing needs and requirements. Evaluating the scalability of security technologies ensures that the organization is prepared to handle future growth and expansion without compromising on security measures.

Another critical factor to consider when evaluating security technologies is the cost-effectiveness of the solutions being implemented. Security professionals must weigh the benefits of investing in new technologies against the potential risks and costs associated with maintaining legacy systems. By conducting a cost-benefit analysis, security professionals can make informed decisions about which technologies to prioritize during the integration process.

Ultimately, evaluating security technologies requires a comprehensive understanding of the organization's security needs, existing systems, and future goals. By taking a strategic and proactive approach to evaluating security technologies, professionals in project management, mergers and acquisitions, corporate security, and cyber security can ensure a smooth and secure transition during a merger or acquisition.

Integrating Security Tools for Efficiency

In order to ensure the successful integration of security tools during a merger or acquisition, it is essential for professionals in project management, corporate security, and cyber security to work together seamlessly. By collaborating effectively, these teams can streamline processes, enhance efficiency, and mitigate potential risks. This subchapter will explore strategies for integrating security tools for efficiency, with a focus on coordinating efforts between corporate security and cyber security teams.

One key aspect of integrating security tools for efficiency is to establish clear communication channels between corporate security and cyber security teams. By fostering open and transparent communication, these teams can effectively share information, identify potential vulnerabilities, and align on security priorities. This collaboration is crucial for ensuring that all security tools are effectively integrated and that potential gaps are addressed promptly.

Another important consideration when integrating security tools for efficiency is to manage the transition of security policies and procedures effectively. During a merger or acquisition, it is common for security policies and procedures to vary between organizations. By developing a comprehensive plan for aligning and consolidating these policies, security professionals can ensure a smooth transition and minimize disruptions to security operations.

Furthermore, project managing the assessment and evaluation of security risks during a merger or acquisition is essential for identifying potential threats and vulnerabilities. By conducting thorough risk assessments, security professionals can prioritize security measures, allocate resources effectively, and implement targeted security solutions. This proactive approach can help to safeguard sensitive data and protect critical assets during the integration process.

Lastly, implementing a comprehensive security training program for employees post-merger is crucial for promoting a culture of security awareness and compliance. By providing employees with the necessary knowledge and skills to identify and respond to security threats, organizations can strengthen their overall security posture and reduce the risk of security incidents. This training program should be tailored to the specific needs of each organization and should include hands-on exercises, simulations, and real-world scenarios to ensure practical application of security best practices. By following these best practices and strategies, professionals in project management, corporate security, and cyber security can effectively integrate security tools for efficiency and ensure the security of their organization's assets during a merger or acquisition.

Upgrading Security Systems for Enhanced Protection

In the fast-paced world of mergers and acquisitions, upgrading security systems is essential to ensure enhanced protection for organizations. As security professionals, it is crucial to understand the importance of integrating corporate security and cyber security teams during a merger or acquisition. By aligning these two departments, organizations can create a robust security framework that addresses potential vulnerabilities and threats effectively.

Project managing the integration of cyber security systems post-merger requires careful planning and coordination. It is essential to assess the existing systems of both organizations and identify areas that need improvement or consolidation. By implementing best practices for coordinating security efforts between corporate and cyber security teams, organizations can streamline communication and collaboration, ultimately enhancing overall security posture.

One of the key challenges during a merger or acquisition is ensuring data security. To address this issue, security professionals must develop strategies to safeguard sensitive information and prevent data breaches. By managing the transition of security policies and procedures, organizations can mitigate risks and maintain compliance with industry regulations.

As part of the integration process, implementing a comprehensive security training program for employees is vital. By educating staff on security best practices and protocols post-merger, organizations can reduce the likelihood of security incidents and enhance overall security awareness. Project managing the consolidation of security technology and tools is also crucial to optimize resources and ensure seamless operations.

In conclusion, mastering project management in mergers and acquisitions requires a strategic approach to security. By upgrading security systems, integrating security teams, and implementing effective communication strategies, organizations can enhance protection and mitigate risks during a merger or acquisition. Security professionals play a critical role in safeguarding organizational assets and ensuring a smooth transition post-merger. By following best practices and leveraging industry expertise, security departments can effectively manage security risks and maintain a secure environment for all stakeholders.

Chapter 10: Strategies for Effective Communication and Collaboration between Security Teams

Establishing Communication Channels

Establishing effective communication channels is crucial in successfully managing mergers and acquisitions, especially when it comes to the security departments involved. For professionals in project management, mergers and acquisitions, corporate security, and cyber security, clear and open lines of communication are essential for coordinating efforts, sharing information, and addressing security concerns during this complex process.

One key aspect of establishing communication channels is ensuring that all relevant stakeholders are identified and included in the communication plan. This includes members of the corporate security team, cyber security team, project management team, and other key individuals involved in the merger or acquisition. By creating a comprehensive list of stakeholders and determining the appropriate communication methods for each group, teams can ensure that important information is disseminated efficiently and effectively.

In addition to identifying stakeholders, it is important to establish regular communication protocols to keep all team members informed and engaged throughout the merger or acquisition process. This may include setting up regular meetings, creating communication schedules, and utilizing collaboration tools to facilitate information sharing. By establishing clear guidelines for communication, teams can prevent misunderstandings, ensure alignment on project goals, and foster a sense of unity among security professionals.

Furthermore, integrating corporate security teams during a merger or acquisition requires a strategic approach to communication. Security professionals must work together to assess security risks, evaluate existing security systems, and develop a plan for integrating security measures post-merger. By establishing communication channels between corporate security teams, cyber security teams, and project management teams, security professionals can effectively coordinate efforts and address security concerns in a timely manner.

Ultimately, effective communication and collaboration between security teams are essential for ensuring data security, managing the transition of security policies and procedures, and consolidating security technology and tools post-merger. By implementing best practices for coordinating security efforts, project managing the assessment of security risks, and implementing comprehensive security training programs for employees, security professionals can mitigate security threats and protect sensitive information during the merger or acquisition process. Through strategic communication and collaboration, security professionals can navigate the complexities of mergers and acquisitions with confidence and success.

Encouraging Collaboration among Security Teams

Encouraging collaboration among security teams is essential for the success of any merger or acquisition project. In the fast-paced and high-stakes environment of M&A, it is crucial for professionals in project management, corporate security, and cyber security to work together seamlessly. By fostering a culture of collaboration and open communication, security teams can effectively address risks and challenges that arise during the integration process.

One of the key strategies for encouraging collaboration among security teams is to establish clear roles and responsibilities. By defining the scope of work for each team and setting expectations upfront, confusion and overlap can be minimized. Project managers should facilitate regular meetings and check-ins to ensure that all security teams are aligned on goals and timelines.

Another important aspect of promoting collaboration among security teams is to create opportunities for cross-functional training and knowledge sharing. By providing employees with the tools and resources they need to succeed, teams can work together more effectively to address security threats and vulnerabilities. This can include conducting joint exercises and simulations to test response capabilities and identify areas for improvement.

Effective communication is also critical for fostering collaboration among security teams. Project managers should establish regular channels for sharing updates, progress reports, and potential risks. By keeping all stakeholders informed and engaged, security teams can work together proactively to address issues before they escalate.

Overall, encouraging collaboration among security teams requires a proactive and strategic approach. By setting clear goals, providing training and resources, and fostering open communication, project managers can help security professionals in corporate security and cyber security work together effectively during a merger or acquisition. This collaboration is essential for ensuring the security and success of the integration process.

Resolving Communication Breakdowns in Security Projects

In the fast-paced world of mergers and acquisitions, communication breakdowns can often occur, especially when it comes to security projects. As professionals in project management, Mergers and acquisitions, Corporate Security, and Cyber Security, it is crucial to understand how to effectively resolve these breakdowns to ensure the success of the project.

One key strategy for resolving communication breakdowns in security projects is to establish clear lines of communication from the outset. This means clearly defining roles and responsibilities within the security team, as well as setting up regular meetings to discuss progress, challenges, and any potential roadblocks. By fostering open communication channels, teams can address issues in a timely manner and prevent misunderstandings from escalating.

Additionally, it is important for project managers to actively listen to the concerns and feedback of team members. By creating a culture of open dialogue and feedback, project managers can gain valuable insights into potential communication breakdowns and work collaboratively with team members to address them. This also helps to build trust and rapport within the team, leading to stronger working relationships and more effective communication overall.

Another effective strategy for resolving communication breakdowns in security projects is to establish clear goals and objectives for the project. By clearly defining what needs to be accomplished and setting measurable targets, teams can stay focused and aligned on the project's objectives. This helps to minimize confusion and miscommunication, as team members are all working towards the same end goal.

Furthermore, project managers should leverage technology and tools to facilitate communication and collaboration within the security team. Whether it's using project management software, messaging platforms, or virtual meeting tools, technology can help streamline communication processes and ensure that team members are always on the same page. By embracing technology, project managers can overcome communication barriers and keep the project on track.

In conclusion, resolving communication breakdowns in security projects requires proactive communication, active listening, clear goal-setting, and leveraging technology. By implementing these strategies, professionals in project management, Mergers and acquisitions, Corporate Security, and Cyber Security can effectively navigate the complexities of security projects during mergers and acquisitions, ensuring a successful outcome for all stakeholders involved.

Conclusion: Mastering Project Management in Mergers and Acquisitions for Security Professionals

In conclusion, mastering project management in mergers and acquisitions for security professionals is essential for ensuring a smooth transition and successful integration of security teams during these complex processes. By following best practices and strategies outlined in this guide, professionals in project management, mergers and acquisitions, corporate security, and cyber security can effectively coordinate and manage security efforts throughout the merger or acquisition process.

Integrating corporate security teams during a merger or acquisition requires careful planning and communication to ensure a seamless transition. By implementing a comprehensive security training program for employees post-merger and managing the consolidation of security technology and tools, security professionals can streamline operations and enhance overall security measures.

Project managing the integration of cyber security systems post-merger is critical for safeguarding sensitive data and preventing security breaches. Strategies for ensuring data security during a merger or acquisition include assessing and evaluating security risks, implementing secure communication channels, and establishing clear security policies and procedures.

Effective communication and collaboration between corporate and cyber security teams is key to successfully coordinating security efforts during a merger or acquisition. By managing the transition of security policies and procedures, security professionals can align security protocols and ensure compliance with regulatory requirements.

In conclusion, mastering project management in mergers and acquisitions for security professionals requires a strategic approach, attention to detail, and effective coordination between corporate and cyber security teams. By following the guidelines and best practices outlined in this guide, security professionals can navigate the complexities of mergers and acquisitions with confidence and ensure the protection of valuable assets and sensitive information.

References

In order to effectively navigate the complex landscape of mergers and acquisitions within the realm of security management, it is essential for professionals in project management, corporate security, and cyber security to have a solid foundation of references to draw upon. This subchapter titled "References" serves as a comprehensive guide for professionals seeking to master the intricacies of project managing mergers and acquisitions within the security domain.

One key aspect of project managing mergers and acquisitions for security professionals is the integration of corporate security teams during the transition process. By referencing best practices and case studies in this area, security professionals can gain valuable insights into how to successfully merge security teams and ensure a seamless transition for all stakeholders involved.

Another critical reference point for security professionals is the project management of integrating cyber security systems post-merger. By leveraging industry standards, guidelines, and expert advice, security professionals can develop a strategic approach to integrating cyber security systems that effectively safeguards critical assets and data throughout the merger and acquisition process.

References also play a vital role in guiding security professionals on strategies for ensuring data security during a merger or acquisition. By referencing industry reports, regulatory requirements, and security frameworks, professionals can develop robust data security measures that mitigate risks and protect sensitive information from potential threats.

Furthermore, references provide valuable insights into best practices for coordinating security efforts between corporate and cyber security teams during a merger or acquisition. By drawing upon established methodologies, tools, and frameworks, security professionals can foster effective communication and collaboration between security teams, leading to a cohesive and unified security strategy post-merger.

In conclusion, the subchapter on "References" serves as a valuable resource for security professionals seeking to excel in project managing mergers and acquisitions within the security domain. By leveraging the insights, best practices, and guidance provided in this subchapter, professionals can navigate the complexities of mergers and acquisitions with confidence and ensure the security of critical assets and data throughout the transition process.

www.ingramcontent.com/pod-product-compliance
Lightning Source LLC
Chambersburg PA
CBHW081021240526
45471CB00018B/3941